To Our Supporters

La Perle Restaurant & Lounge Everett, MA

La Bootik East Meadow, NY

Legal Blend East Meadow, NY

Bon Appetit Restaurant Dorchester Center, MA

To Our Family

Derosiers Laguerre Lherisson Saint-Aubin McBryde

Desert Eliacin Auguste

Thank You!

#WOWHAITI #WOWAYITI

The Spirit Of Haiti

FROM THE CREATIVE TEAM LEAD

Dear Reader,

The purpose of this project is to share Haitian heritage and its story in a unique, concise, and vivid way. Collectively we wanted to provide a book and digital resource that would serve anyone looking to explore what it means to be of Haitian descent. Personally, I wanted to be able to share something with my children that would help them understand my cultural point of view and where their grandma is from.

C. Desert, a friend since college, shared the vision. We toyed around with a variety of Haitian media and content ideas. Finally we landed on the idea of a mostly visual book. The informational texts in this book are the result of internet searches, conversations with friends, and family in our network. There are facts, legends, stories and interpretations highlighted in this text. We use QR Codes to deepen the experience with unique visuals, audio, and merch.

Finally, the Haitian story is rich, complex and iconic. We could not fit it all in one book but my personal goal was to deliver a place to start on a variety of topics. I believe we accomplished just that. We hope you find this book honest, prideful, and shareable. May it serve you well!

Thank you,

THE SPIRIT OF
HAITI

DESIGN &
CURATION.

L. Derosiers

C. Desert

CONSULT &
SUPPORT.

M. Derosiers

S. Lys

A. Germain

McBryde Books, LLC

+

People & Culture. Page 6

History | Stories & Legends Page 18

The Landmarks. Page 42

Proverbs. Page 64

Essential Recipes. Page 82

WELCOME

MOUN YO, AK KILTI A
UNION FE LA FORCE

PEOPLE & CULTURE

#WOWHAITI #WOWAYITI

HAITIANS
& THE DIASPORA

Haitian culture is a rich blend of African, French, Spanish, and indigenous influences. Shaped by strong spirited people, Haitians are warm in hospitality. They are also vibrant in art and cuisine. Haitian diaspora are all over the world and have large communities in the USA. This includes, Florida, New York Tri State, & Boston areas.

Creativity permeates every part of life. Intricate crafts, and lively celebrations embody the identity. Haitian music, dance, and food can be described as rich, bold, and soulful. The heartbeat of Haitian culture resonates in the rhythms of compass and rara music, the graceful movements of traditional dances, and the flavorsome dishes like griot and diri ak djon djon.

A deep-rooted spirituality adds even more layers to the culture, reflecting a people who continuously find strength and unity in faith and heritage.

VARIOUS COMMUNITIES AROUND THE WORLD

Haitian Island Population - 11 Million (approx.)
Haitian Diaspora - 3.5 Million (Estimated)
USA - 1 MIL, Chile - 200k, Canada - 200k
Dominican - 800k, Brazil - 150k
Bahamas - 80k, Mexico - 70k, France - 60k

THE PEOPLE & CULTURE
UNITY MAKES STRENGTH

Celebs of Haitian Decent

USA'S TOP CHARTING ARTIST OF HAITIAN HERITAGE

Wyclef Jean stands as one of the most prominent Haitian-American artist to top the charts in the United States. He gained fame as a founding member of the hip-hop group The Fugees. Their album "The Score" became a massive success in the mid-1990s, producing hits like "Killing Me Softly" and "Ready or Not". But there has be a long standing presence of Haitian influence in American music business and culture. Here are some of the more recognizable names.

| Wyclef Jean

| Kaytranada

| Kodak Black

| Jason Derulo

| Maxwell

ART & FILM INDUSTRY | MAINSTREAM & INDIE SUCCESS

Haitian artists and filmmakers have etched their mark on the global stage, infusing their creativity with a rich cultural POV. From the thought-provoking documentaries of Raoul Peck, to the literary prowess of Edwidge Danticat, and the impactful visual art of figures like Jean-Michel Basquiat, whose vibrant works reflect societal struggles and cultural identity.

| Jean-Michel Basquiat

| Garcelle Beauvais

| Raoul Peck

| Edwidge Danticat

| Michaëlle Jean

SPORTS & WORLD CLASS ATHLETICS

Haitian athletes have left an indelible mark in various sports. Figures like Samuel Dalembert, a skilled basketball player known for his defensive prowess in the NBA, and Pierre Garçon, a dynamic wide receiver in the NFL, have represented Haiti's athletic excellence. Born to Japanese mother and Haitian father, Naomi Osaka's tennis excellence is a testament those with Haitian ancestry. Soccer players such as Jean Jacques Pierre and Wilde-Donald Guerrier have captivated audiences with their skill and dedication, contributing significantly to their national teams and clubs worldwide.

| Naomi Osaka - Pro Tennis

| Karl-Anthony Towns NBA

| Samuel Dalembert NBA

| Jason Pierre-Paul NFL

| Pierre Garçon NFL

FAMOUS STARS ON THE HAITIAN ISLAND

Outside of the country's presidents and politicians, several notable Haitians have made significant strides in entertainment, academia, and social impact.. These leaders exemplify the intersection of business and social responsibility. They leverage their influence and resources to uplift Haitian communities.

| Michel Martelly - Singer

| Emeline Michel - Singer

| Pasteur Gregory Toussaint

| Manno Charlemagne - Singer

| Lumane Casimir - Singer

HAITIANS OF POP CULTURE

EWO NAN ESPÒ KARAYIB

A HAITIAN SPORTS STORY

World Cup 1974
A WIN FOR HAITI & THE CARIBBEAN

Haiti's men's national football team, also known as "Les Grenadiers," last appeared in the FIFA World Cup in 1974. The tournament was held in West Germany (now Germany). In that World Cup, Haiti made history by becoming the first Caribbean team to qualify for the FIFA World Cup. During the tournament Haiti competed in Group 4 alongside Italy, Poland, and Argentina. Although they didn't advance past the group stage, Haiti's participation in the 1974 World Cup was a significant achievement, showcasing the potential and talent within the Caribbean football landscape.

Haiti was the underdog and not expected to have a chance. When the first half ended tied at zero the crowd became high tension. It was a moral win for the country. At the beginning of the second half Italy and rest of the world were stunned. A goal made by Emmanuel Sanno erupted the Caribbean with pride! Though the match was ultimately lost to Italy, scoring and leading against the Italy was recognition. Like their revolutionary story, the Haitians stamped themselves as worthy competitors in the world arena.

Arsène Auguste

On behalf of the Auguste & Eliacin families, we would like to honor Arsène Auguste (aka. Pèlao). He was part of the Haitian national team in 1974. A world class athlete, Auguste played in 15 World Cup qualifying matches from 1973-1981.

SPORTS HERO OF CARIBBEAN

DILIAN KREYÒL

Kreyòl

LANGUAGES SPOKEN

THE NATIVE TONGUE

Haitian Creole, known locally as Kreyòl, is a language spoken by the majority of Haitians. General research says that this language developed from interactions between African slaves and European colonizers (primarily French), during Haiti's colonial period. It has its roots in West African languages, including the Fon, Ewe, and Yoruba, along with influences from indigenous Caribbean languages. Kreyòl is an essential part of Haitian culture and identity, serving as the default language for communication among Haitians in various spheres of life, including government, education, and everyday conversation. French is the second most used language on the island. It is often used in formal situations. English and Spanish are also common in Haiti. They are utilized by the more migrant population and in areas near Haitian - Dominican boarder.

SAY IT IN CREOLE

HAITIAN MUSIC

Popular Styles of Music

Kompa (Compas): Considered Haiti's national music, Kompa is rhythmic dance music characterized by a pulsating beat, guitar-driven melodies, and brass instruments. It originated in the late 1950s and has evolved over time, blending influences from African rhythms, merengue, and jazz. **Notable Bands:** Tabou Combo, System Band, Carimi.

Rara: Rooted in Vodou traditions, Rara music is played during festive processions and celebrations, particularly during the Lenten season leading up to Easter. It features percussions, horns, and call-and-response vocals, creating a spiritual musical experience. **Notable Bands:** Boukman Eksperyans , RAM.

Twoubadou: With acoustic guitar-driven melodies and ballad-like songs, Twoubadou music often tells stories of love, everyday life, and social issues. With a relaxed and soulful sound. **Notable Artists:** Manno Charlemagne, Ti Corn, Raymond Cajuste.

Mizik Rasin: Translating to "roots music," Mizik Rasin incorporates traditional Haitian elements, African rhythms, and modern sounds. It often involves the use of traditional drums.

Haitian Hip-Hop (Rap Kreyòl): Rap Kreyòl blends elements of hip-hop with Haitian Creole lyrics, addressing social issues, politics, and everyday life in Haiti. **Notable Artist:** Fantôm, Wendy, Izolan, King Posse.

HERE COMES THE WHINE (GYRATION)

Products Of Haiti

HAITIAN VETIVER | MENS & WOMENS FRAGRANCES

Vetiver is a prized aromatic essential oil produced from the roots of Vetiveria zizanioides, a grass native to Haiti. Renowned for its unique, earthy fragrance, Haitian vetiver is in high demand in the global fragrance and cosmetics industry. The country's climate and fertile soil create an ideal environment for cultivating vetiver. Its cultivation and distillation provide valuable income opportunities for Haitian farmers and support economic development. Haitian vetiver is not only an aromatic treasure but also a source of livelihood and sustainable growth for local communities. Here are some frangrances that include Haitian Vetiver.

| Tom Ford Grey Vetiver
| Guerlain Vetiver
| Hermès Terre d'Hermès
| Creed Original Vetiver
| Diptyque Vetyverio

CAFE HAITIEN | HAITIAN COFFEE

Haitian coffee is a cherished export known for its rich flavor and unique character. Grown in the high-altitude regions of Haiti, notably the Kenscoff Plateau and the Nord department, this Arabica coffee is renowned for its bright acidity and hints of fruitiness, offering a delightful and distinctive taste. While the coffee industry in Haiti faces challenges, including natural disasters and limited infrastructure, it continues to attract coffee connoisseurs with its exceptional quality and the potential for sustainable, ethically sourced beans. Haitian coffee stands as a testament to the country's agricultural heritage and the determination of its coffee producers to uphold a tradition that blends the flavors of their mountainous land.

| Rebo Coffee
| La Colombe
| Kafe Pa Nou
| Kahwa Coffee

MANGO |
HAITIAN MANGOS

Haitian mangoes are unique and celebrated for their luscious sweetness and aromatic taste. Haiti is one of the largest mango exporters in the Caribbean. These succulent fruits are grown across the country, from lush valleys to mountainous regions, making them a significant part of the Haitian diet and agricultural output. With a wide variety of mango cultivators, each with its unique taste and texture, Haitian mangoes are not only a delicious treat but also an essential source of income for many local farmers.

BIÈ |
PRESTIGE BEER

Prestige, the flagship beer of Haiti, has an enduring history that mirrors the country. Founded in the 1970s by Michel Handal, a Salvadoran entrepreneur, Brasserie Nationale d'Haïti was established. Facing logistical challenges & adversity in post-dictatorship Haiti, the brewery persevered, and Prestige quickly became a symbol of Haitian pride.

CLAIRIN |
BARBANCOURT & SAMAROL

Haitian rum production is a time-honored tradition dating back centuries, showcasing the country's expertise in crafting fine spirits. Haiti's sugarcane plantations are the primary source of the high-quality cane juice used in rum-making. One of the most celebrated Haitian rums is Clairin, a strong, artisanal, and traditional spirit known for its complex and rich flavors. Age-old methods, such as natural fermentation and pot still distillation, are used to create rums. Haitian rum has gained international recognition.

LWIL MASKRETI |
HAITIAN CASTOR OIL

Haitian castor oil is highly sought after in the cosmetics and beauty industries due to its numerous applications for hair and skin care. Derived from the seeds of the castor plant (Ricinus communis), it has been cultivated in Haiti for generations. Rich in essential fatty acids, it's believed to promote hair growth, hydrate the skin, and even alleviate certain ailments. The production of castor oil in Haiti often follows traditional methods, emphasizing purity and organic cultivation.

MADE IN HAITI

AY-TI

HISTORY

TIME PERIOD
700 AD - 1492

#WOWHAITI #WOWAYITI

The Indigenous Culture

Haiti's indigenous culture is predominantly rooted in the Taíno heritage. The island's original inhabitants infused their daily lives with reverence for nature, spirituality, and intricate craftsmanship seen in their pottery and art. Their legacy endures in the language, culinary delight (like cassava bread), and folklore that weave through present day Haitian traditions.

Original Names

The indigenous of Haiti and surrounding islands had several names for the Haitian Island. The name "Haiti" is rooted in the Taino name "Ay-Ti". This is believed to mean "Flower of High Land" or "Land of High Mountains".

Haiti aka
Bohio, Quisqueya, Ayiti

TAINO KINGDOM

Marién · Magua · Maguana · Higüey · Jaragua

HAITI

HISTORY, ICONS, & LEGENDS

Anacaona

Anacaona Ayizini, was a prominent Taíno queen and poet in pre-Columbus Haiti. She was of the indigenous Taino people and born around 1474 in the chiefdom of Xaragua. Anacaona was known for her wisdom and talent as a composer of songs and poetry. She was reigning queen of her people and sought to promote peace and prosperity on the island.

During her lifetime Ayiti was invaded and colonized by Spanish explorers. The arrival of Christopher Columbus to Ayiti was the start of an era that included extreme brutality, forced labor, and enslavement. Anacaona used her position as a queen to protect and support her people as much as she could. Unfortunately Her efforts at peaceful coexistence were in vain.

In 1503, the Spanish governor invited Anacaona and other Taíno leaders to a feast in peace, but it was a trap. The execution of the poet chieftess set the tone for Taino and Transatlantic Africans relations with the Spanish. The message was clear, there could be no peaceful coexistence.

IT'S ON LONG ROADS THAT YOU LEARN YOUR STRENGTH.

REVOLUTION

TIME PERIOD 1791 – 1804

The First Black Republic

Haiti's history is marked by power struggles, revolts, remarkable fortitude and brilliant expressions. From the arrival of European explorers, to the brutality of colonization, and the ground breaking revolution, this island nation has endured a tumultuous journey toward independence.

The world's first Black republic, Haiti, is a testament to the best and worst of our world civilization. Haitian people represent the strength, unwavering spirit, and the enduring legacy of breaking chains to claim freedom. Here are some of Haiti's historical icons in order of timeline..

*LÈ OU GEN WÒCH NAN MEN OU, OU PA PÈ CHEN."

Toussaint Louverture

"The Black Napoleon"

François-Dominique Toussaint was born a slave on May 20, 1743 in Saint-Domingue (present-day Haiti). The island was then a French colony known for its brutal slave system and lucrative sugar industry. Despite his enslavement, Toussaint learned to read and write and acquired knowledge of medicinal plants and military strategy. He was granted his freedom in 1776.

In 1791, the Haitian Revolution erupted when enslaved Africans and Afro-descendant people rebelled against their oppressors. Toussaint quickly emerged as a leader in this rebellion, demonstrating exceptional military and organisational skills. This earned him the nickname "The Black Napoleon". Today he is known as an icon of Haiti's soveriengty, and for writing the first constitution. Though captured by the French and imprisoned, the torch was passed to his fellow freedom fighter Dessaline.

CONSTITUTION OF 1801

Haiti's first constitution, established in 1801 under the leadership of Toussaint Louverture, was a ground breaking document that embodied the principles of liberty and equality. Some key highlights include:

Abolition of Slavery: The constitution abolished slavery and granted freedom to all enslaved individuals in Haiti, making it the first country in the world to officially declare the end of slavery.

Equal Rights: It proclaimed equality among all citizens regardless of race or color, providing a stark departure from the deeply entrenched racial hierarchies prevalent in many other nations at the time.

Land Redistribution: The constitution also addressed land redistribution, aiming to distribute land to formerly enslaved individuals, offering them the means for economic autonomy and independence.

Establishment of Leadership: It established Toussaint Louverture as governor-general for life, recognizing his leadership during the revolution against French colonial rule.

Affirmation of Sovereignty: The constitution affirmed Haiti's sovereignty and independence, asserting the nation's right to self-governance and self-determination.

WHEN YOU HAVE A STONE IN YOUR HAND, YOU'RE NOT AFRAID OF DOGS

AFRICAN LEGEND & LINEAGE

Victora Montou aka Toya

Toya was a west African Dahomey warrior who was betrayed and sold into slavery. She was brought to the island St. Domingue where she met a young Dessaline. Legend has it that his mother entrusted the young boy to her when she passed.

Toya is said to have tutored and joined Desssaline in battle. He considered her an aunt and took care of her in her old age. Integral to the success of the Haitian Revolution, Toya in other women of Haitian history are the roots from where the Haitian women's strength, resilience, and commitment are securely planted.

Tribal Lineages Of Haitian People

Akan: From present-day Ghana and Ivory Coast.
Yoruba: Primarily from Nigeria, Benin, and Togo.
Igbo: Mainly from southeastern Nigeria.
Fon: From Benin.
Ewe: From Togo and Ghana.
Mande peoples: Spanning across countries like Mali, Guinea, Senegal, and the Ivory Coast.

The Wakanda Connection

Wakanda's hero, T'Challa, has been depicted as having a significant connection to Haiti through his mother, Ramonda. Ramonda, in some storylines, is portrayed as having Haitian ancestry, thus creating a familial tie between Black Panther and Haiti.

The marvel film adds loose connections through the Dahomey inspired " Dora Milaje" who's leader could be a reflection of " Toya". Her support of the Black panther is similar to that of Toya's support of Dessaline. Lastly, the film ends in a depiction of present day Haiti and an intro to T'Challa's son named "Toussaint".

27

LIVE TODAY BUT...
REMEMBER THERE'S A TOMORROW

More Iconic Women Of The Haitian Revolution...

SI OU VLE MANJE BON MIEL, OU PA PE PIKAN ZÈG.

Women were integral to the success of the Haitian rebellion. Many took up arms and fought alongside their male counterparts. Meanwhile others, such as Suzanne Béliar and Marie-Claire Heureuse Félicité, used their influence to provide crucial support, intelligence, and medical aid.

Défilée-La-Folle The "Mad Woman"

Marie-Jeanne Lamartinière

Marie-Jeanne's role in the revolution became notable as she joined the rebel forces and distinguished herself as a courageous and strategic military leader. She earned the respect of fellow soldiers. The Battle of Crête-à-Pierrot in 1802 was one of her most significant moments. She led a resistance defending the fortress and inflicted heavy casualties to the French.

IF YOU WANT TO EAT GOOD HONEY, YOU CAN'T BE AFRAID OF THE BEE'S STING

Female Leadership
A Heritage of Strong Women

Cécile Fatiman

Fatiman was a Vodou priestess and freedom fighter. Along with Dutty Boukman she led a Vodou ceremony at Bwa Kayiman in 1791, and is believed to have played a crucial role in inciting the slave rebellion that ultimately led to Haitian independence. Her spiritual guidance and influence were instrumental in inspiring the enslaved population to rise up against their oppressors.

Catherine Flon

Catherine Flon is a celebrated figure in Haitian history and is particularly known for her role in the creation of the Haitian flag. She is said to have sewn together the first Haitian flag, which was composed of blue and red horizontal stripes. The blue symbolized the African ancestry of the Haitian people, while the red represented the bloodshed during the struggle for independence.

DON'T GIVE WHAT YOU HAVE, GIVE WHAT YOU CAN

SE NAN CHEMEN

LWEN OU KA APRANN FÒS OU

Jean-Jacques Dessaline *The Liberator Of Haiti*

Also born a slave, It is said that early in his life he was in care of a dahomey warrior woman (Toya) who was transplanted in Haiti through slavery. Legend has it she taught him about battle and groomed him as a leader. Dessalines rose to prominence in the military alongside Toussaint Louverture.

After Louverture's capture, Dessalines continued the fight for Haitian independence, and in 1804, he beat the French forces and declared Haiti the first independent black republic in the world. Dessalines became the first ruler of independent Haiti, taking on the title of Emperor.

His leadership was effective and needed to win but his strong authorization rule lead to tensions and his assassination in 1806. Despite his controversial legacy, Dessalines remains a symbol of Haitian resistance and liberty

Soup Joumou is known as "Independence Soup" and is a cherished culinary tradition deeply intertwined with the history of Haitian independence. You will find simple recipies in the dedicated culinary section of this book.

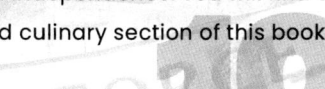

1804

IT'S ON LONGER PATHS THAT YOU LEARN YOUR STRENGTH

King of The North

Christophe became a prominent figure in the newly formed nation. He initially served as a general in the army of Jean-Jacques Dessalines. However, tensions arose between Dessalines and Christophe, leading to Dessalines' assassination in 1806. Following Dessalines' death, Haiti was divided into two separate states, with Christophe ruling in the north as President and later as King.

King Henri I's rule was marked by discontent and opposition, particularly from the mulatto population in the south of Haiti, who resented his autocratic governance. Additionally, economic challenges and disputes with foreign powers further strained his rule.

In 1820, Henri Christophe faced a revolt in his kingdom, which led to his eventual abdication and exile. Fearing capture and humiliation, he died by suicide on October 8, 1820.

Henri Christophe

THE KINGDOM

Alexandre Pétion

Leader of The South

Alexandre Pétion was a leader of mixed-race descent who held more liberal and decentralized political views influenced by Enlightenment ideals. Pétion's government was characterized by principles of democracy, land distribution to former enslaved individuals, and social equality. Pétion's rule emphasized education, and he supported institutions that promoted these values. He also played a role in the development of Haiti's flag and coat of arms.

Pétion's administration, however, was marked by financial difficulties and political instability. He faced challenges from rival leaders and regional conflicts. Pétion died in 1818, and his death marked a period of political uncertainty in the southern part of Haiti, as different leaders vied for power.

THE REPUBLIC

TWO BULLS CAN'T REMAIN ON THEE SAME PLAIN.

Liberating Latin America

After gaining their freedom through a long and arduous revolution against French colonial rule, Haitian leaders, including Toussaint Louverture and Jean-Jacques Dessalines, supported and welcomed refugees and freedom fighters from other regions, including South America. They provided refuge, military assistance, and inspiration to individuals fighting against colonial powers and slavery.

In the early 19th century, Haiti helped many countries gain their independence, including: Northwest Brazil, Guyana, Venezuela, Ecuador, Colombia, Panama, Northern Peru, Costa Rica, Nicaragua, Bolivia. One notable instance is the assistance provided to Simón Bolívar, the Venezuelan military and political leader who played a crucial role in South America's fight for independence from Spanish colonial rule. Bolívar sought support from Haiti, receiving aid in the form of weapons, supplies, and even troops from President Alexandre Pétion, the then-ruler of Haiti. This aid from Haiti was instrumental in bolstering Bolívar's efforts in the fight against Spanish rule in parts of South America.

While Haiti's direct involvement in freeing South American slaves was limited, its existence as a free Black republic and its support for liberation movements served as a beacon of hope and inspiration for oppressed people globally, including those fighting for freedom in South America. The Haitian Revolution's impact extended far beyond its borders, influencing and encouraging movements for liberty and equality in other parts of the world.

Little Known FACTS...

- Haitian soldiers fought alongside Americans to gain independence in the America Revolutionary War, between September 19 and October 18, 1779, in Savannah, Georgia.

- Haiti was the biggest manufacturer and exporter of baseballs by the 1970's after Rawlings acquired its first plant in 1969 (up until 1987).

- The city of Chicago was founded by Jean Baptiste Point DuSable, a Haitian pioneer trader, around 1780.

- Haiti took a stance against Nazi Germany by issuing life-saving visas to Jewish refugees during WWII. Some of these refugees remained in Haiti where their descendants still live.

- The Louisiana Purchase was heavily influenced by the financial burden of the Haitian Revolution on France. The French were forced to sell to the United States.

- The term "Zoe" is used in refference to a Haitian person. Meaning " Bone" in kreyol, it is a way of conveying strength and pride by saying Haitians are "hard to the bone". Zoe pound is a street gang in Maimi, FL that started as organized protection for Haitians being harassed. For this reason the term Zoe took on deeper meaning in Haitian & American street culture.

Arrested Development

Haiti's development since the time of Presidents Alexandre Pétion and Henri Christophe, who both passed away in the early 19th century, has been marked by significant challenges and progress. In the years following their leadership, the nation has faced political instability, foreign intervention, and economic struggles. President Jean-Pierre Boyer successfully unified north and south but entered a devastating agreement with the French to pay reparations for lost land and business on the island. From this point the country's history includes periods of dictatorship, coups, occupation and natural disasters that have hindered sustained growth.

The country has seen improvements in healthcare and education, with increased access to primary education. Additionally, Haiti's vibrant art and culture continue to gain international recognition, attracting tourists and contributing to the nation's economy. Efforts to strengthen governance and reduce corruption have also been ongoing, though progress in these areas has been uneven. International aid and cooperation have played a dual sided role in Haiti's development. Though efforts and resources are committed to Haiti it is commonly understood that these resources do not trickle down to the people and the corruption that hurts Haiti likely runs deep in and outside of the country's borders.

Political Struggles & Corruption

The regime of François "Papa Doc" Duvalier in Haiti, lasted from 1957 until his death in 1971. While there were some developments in infrastructure and social programs under Papa Doc's rule, during his time in power political opposition was brutally suppressed. A pervasive system of informants, known as the Tonton Macoutes, maintained control through fear and violence. Jean-Claude Duvalier, also known as "Baby Doc," was the ruler of Haiti from 1971 to 1986, succeeding his father. It is said that he was influenced and controlled by his fathers peers and colleagues during his time. Tensions rose under the harsh rule and accusations of embezzlement of state funds. In 1986, public discontent and international pressure forced Duvalier into exile, bringing an end to his family's nearly 30-year authoritarian rule.

THE OWNER KNOWS WHERE THE HOUSE IS BROKEN.

Story of Foreign Interventions

Columbus's arrival in the Caribbean in 1492 marked the beginning of European colonization in the Americas, leading to the transatlantic African slave trade, and the spread of diseases that had a catastrophic impact on the indigenous population.

The French impact on Haiti's development has been significant and complex. Its economic exploitation through extreme system slavery made Haiti (Saint Domingue) one of the most profitable colonies. Post rebellion the French culture had a lasting impact in areas of language, legal systems, architecture and cuisine. Even social and racial hierarchies translated into independent Haiti. Economic aggression towards Haiti led by France to keep it internationally isolated and suppressed. This included reparations forced on Haiti in exchange for the recognition of its independence.

COLONIZER

CONQUEROR

20 YR OCCUPATION OF HAITI

The U.S. Occupation of Haiti, which lasted from 1915 to 1934, was a pivotal chapter in Haitian history. It began when U.S. Marines landed in Port-au-Prince to restore order in the nation marked by political instability and economic turmoil by this time. While the occupation initially sought to modernize Haiti's infrastructure and institutions, it was marked by mixed results and significant controversy.

On one hand, the occupation introduced important reforms in areas such as public health, education, and infrastructure development. However, it also led to the suppression of Haitians resistance, infringements on sovereignty, and more economic exploitation. The occupation eventually faced criticism from the international community. It came to an end in 1934, leaving a complex legacy in Haitian memory.

Bill Clinton's apology to Haiti came in 2010, following a devastating earthquake that resulted in immense loss of life and widespread destruction. As the United Nations Special Envoy for Haiti, Clinton expressed regret for the role the United States played in undermining Haiti's rice production through trade policies that harmed its domestic agricultural sector. He acknowledged the negative impact this had on Haiti's food security. Clinton's apology was an important recognition.

CAPITALIST

WHEN YOU DRINK WATER, REMEMBER IT'S SOURCE.

10 BEAUTIFUL & HISTORIC LOCATIONS

LANDMARKS

The ISLAND

Located on the western part of the island of Hispaniola (formerly known as St. Domingue), Haiti has a diverse and striking landscape. Its topography showcases a blend of mountains, valleys, and coastal plains. The backbone of the country is the Massif du Nord and the Chaîne de la Selle mountain ranges, housing Haiti's highest peak, Pic La Selle (its name loosely meaning peak of the sky). Steep slopes, deep valleys, and plateaus interlace the landscape, while fertile plains like the Cul-de-Sac and Artibonite Valley sprawl across its terrain. With a mix of tropical forests, mangroves, and stunning coastline, Haiti's land is rich in natural resources.

Haiti also has impressive biodiversity with unique species of plants and animals. It's home to the Hispaniolan solenodon, a rare and ancient mammal found only on the island, a unique and delicious version of mango, rare species of frog and butterflies. Haitian vetiver, castor oil, and coffee are growing commodities in global markets.

This section highlights unique places in the country. Links to videos , and VR content are provided for a imersive look.

The Pearl of The Antilles

SCAN QR CODE
FOR VR, VIDEOS, & MORE IMAGES

UNESCO WORLD HERITAGE SITE   LOCATED IN MILOT, HAITI

HISTORICAL LANDMARK

Citadelle Laferrière

The Citadelle is one of the largest fortresses in the Americas and is often considered an architectural marvel. It covers an area of 10,000 square meters (approximately 2.5 acres) and features towering stone walls that rise to heights of up to 40 meters (130 feet). It has a star-shaped layout and is adorned with various decorative features and symbols, including the image of the Haitian flag and the French motto "Liberté ou la Mort" (Liberty or Death). Situated atop a mountain in the Nord department of Haiti, it offers panoramic views of the surrounding countryside and the Bay of Cap-Haïtien.

SCAN QR CODE FOR VIDEO

46

UNESCO WORLD HERITAGE SITE
LOCATED IN MILOT, HAITI

HISTORICAL LANDMARK

Sans-Souci Palace

The Sans-Souci Palace was designed to be a symbol of the newly independent nation's power and prosperity. It was constructed during the early 19th century between 1810 and 1813 by the order of Henri Christophe the (self-proclaimed) King of Haiti. It was an architectural marvel of its time showcasing a stunning facade, neo classical elements, as well as European and African influences in its design. It is part of a building complex that includes, the Citadelle Laferrière, and the Ramiers plantation.

Unfortunately, the palace fell into disrepair and was damaged by an earthquake in 1842. Today, the ruins along with the nearby Citadelle Laferrière, are UNESCO World Heritage Sites and popular tourist attractions, offering a glimpse into Haiti's past and its role in the fight for independence.

SCAN QR CODE FOR VIDEO

LOCATION — PORT AU PRINCE, HAITI

TOURIST STOP

LABADEE Cruise Stop

Labadie, situated along Haiti's northern coast, is a serene and picturesque destination renowned for its pristine beaches, lush palms, and tranquil atmosphere. This coastal paradise, often visited by cruise ships, offers visitors a chance to bask in the sun on powdery sands, swim in crystal-clear waters, and indulge in various water activities. Labadie also offers glimpses into local Haitian culture through artisan markets and cultural performances, making it a delightful blend of natural beauty and cultural experiences for travellers seeking an escape.

The Labadee cruise port, a private resort leased to Royal Caribbean International, was established as a cruise stop in the late 1980s. Royal Caribbean entered into a long-term lease agreement with the Haitian government to develop Labadee as a port destination for their cruise ships. Since then, Labadee has been a popular stop for cruise itineraries in the Caribbean.

SCAN QR CODE
FOR VIDEO

LOCATION — PORT AU PRINCE, HAITI

ICONIC STATUE

Neg Mawon Statue

Sculpted by Albert Mangonès and erected in Port-au-Prince, this iconic sculpture portrays a triumphant, muscular figure breaking free from chains, representing the struggle against slavery and the fight for independence.

The term "Neg Mawon" or "Maroon" refers to formerly enslaved individuals who escaped and formed communities of freedom fighters. They resisted colonial oppression and sought liberty. This statue commemorates Haiti's history of rebellion and perserverence, honoring the strength and courage of those who fought against slavery and exploitation. It is a symbol of black liberation at a world scale and a potent reminder of the Haitian legacy.

SCAN QR CODE
FOR VIDEO

LOCATION

PORT AU PRINCE, HAITI

THE CAPITAL

PORT-AU-PRINCE

Port-au-Prince, the capital and largest city of Haiti, holds immense importance as the economic, cultural, and political hub of the nation. It serves as the epicenter of commerce, industry, and government, playing a pivotal role in Haiti's history and development. The city's bustling markets, educational institutions, and cultural sites embody the nation's identity. While the city has faced challenges, including natural disasters (Earthquake of 2010) and political instability, its significance in the life of Haiti cannot be understated, making it a central player in the country's past, present, and future.

Use the QR link to take a tour of the city's past and present.

SCAN QR CODE FOR VIDEO

MOUNTAINOUS LANDSCAPE

The Great Mountains

Haiti's mountainous terrain has had significant influence on its agriculture and overall landscape. The country is characterized by two main mountain ranges: the " Massif du Nord" in the north and the "Massif de la Hotte" in the south hence is indigenous name " Ayiti" which is believed to mean " land of high mountains" in taino dialect. Agriculture employs a significant portion of the population. The primary crops include staples like maize, rice, beans, and sweet potatoes. Livestock, such as goats and cattle, are also raised. Haitian coffee, known for its unique flavor and history, is grown in the mountainous regions of the country, particularly in the areas around the Kenscoff Plateau and the Nord region. The coffee is predominantly of the Arabica variety and is often shade-grown, benefiting from the ideal altitude and climate for cultivation.

Much of Haiti's agricultural production takes place in rural areas, with subsistence farmers cultivating small plots of land. These farmers often face challenges such as access to resources, financing, and modern farming techniques. There is a growing interest in sustainable and organic farming practices in Haiti, focusing on preserving the environment and promoting self-sufficiency.

SCAN QR CODE FOR VIDEO

LOCATION JACMEL, HAITI

NATURAL LANDMARK

Bassin Bleu In Jacmel

Bassin Bleu, located in Jacmel, Haiti, is a stunning natural wonder that draws visitors from all over the world. This captivating site is renowned for its vibrant blue pools surrounded by lush tropical foliage. Local legend has it that centuries ago, the Taino princess Anacaona discovered this hidden gem while exploring the wilderness. Struck by the pools' captivating beauty, she named the site after its blue waters that seem to shine especially bright under the Caribbean sun.

SCAN QR CODE FOR VIDEO

LOCATION: CAMP-PERRIN, SUD HAITI

NATURAL LANDMARK

Saut-Mathurine

Situated near the town of Camp-Perrin, Saut-Mathurine is the largest waterfall in Haiti. It plunges over 100 feet into a tranquil pool, offering a majestic spectacle for visitors. Bassin Zim, Cascade Pichon, and Bassin Saint-Jacques are other most noted waterfalls on the island. These waterfalls are not only natural landmarks but also offer visitors the opportunity to explore Haiti's stunning landscapes and enjoy outdoor activities.

Bassin Zim

Cascade Pichon

Bassin Saint-Jacques

SCAN QR CODE FOR VIDEO

LOCATION
MIRAGOÂNEE, HAITI

HISTORICAL LANDMARK

Anacaona Statute & Cave

Sculpted by Albert Mangones, the statue of Anacaona stands as a tribute to the indigenous leader whose legacy echoes through Haiti's history. It is located in the town of Léogâne, Haiti. Anacaona's statue is in regal posture and captures the essence of her leadership and cultural heritage. The Anacaona Cave, nestled in Haiti, is believed to be a place where she sought refuge. It's a sacred site, steeped in legend, where her memory lives on, inviting visitors to connect with the rich heritage and stories of Haiti's past. Both the statue and the cave serve as powerful reminders of Anacaona's enduring legacy and the resilience of Haiti's indigenous roots amidst the passage of time.

SCAN QR CODE FOR VIDEO

62

LOCATION
CAP-HAITIEN, HAITI

HISTORICAL LANDMARK

Cap-Haitien Cathedral

The Cap-Haitien Cathedral, also known as the Cathedral of Our Lady of the Assumption, is a historic landmark in Cap-Haitien, Haiti, revered for its architectural splendor and spiritual significance. Constructed in the 18th century, this grand cathedral showcases a captivating blend of Baroque and neoclassical styles, characterized by its graceful arches and ornate detailing. Throughout its history, the cathedral has weathered natural disasters and restoration efforts, standing as a testament to resilience and faith within the local community. Its towering presence in Cap-Haitien continues to serve as a revered sanctuary for worshipers. There are several notable cathedrals in Haiti.

Cathedral of Our Lady of the Assumption,
Sacred Heart Church (Port-au-Prince)
Cathedral of Cap-Haïtien
Notre-Dame-du-Perpétuel-Secours (Cap-Haitien)
Eglise St. Pierre (pétion-Ville)
Cathedral of St. James

SCAN QR CODE FOR VIDEO

PROVERBS

PROVERBS, SAYINGS & ILLUSTRATIONS

HAITIAN WORDS OF WISDOM

Haitian proverbs and sayings offer wisdom, insight, and often a touch of humor. Passed down through generations, these proverbs reflect the perseverance, spirituality, and resourcefulness of the Haitian people. They simplify life's complexities and offer succinct yet profound lessons. They are not just words but echoes of history, culture, and the collective wisdom of a spirited people.

SCAN QR CODE FOR AUDIO & ILLUSTRATIONS

PROVERBS, SAYINGS & ILLUSTRATIONS

Bonjou w se paspò ou.
"Your greeting is your passport..."

A warm and friendly greeting can take you places and open doors. Remember, you only get as far as the people you are willing to talk to.

Bay kou, bliye; pote mak, sonje.
"Give a blow, it's forgotten; receive a blow and it's remembered."

The attacker tends to forget the hurt they have caused. The victim remembers and is often motivated by it.

SCAN QR CODE FOR AUDIO & ILLUSTRATIONS

PROVERBS, SAYINGS & ILLUSTRATIONS

Deye mon, gen mon.
"Behind the mountain, there are mountains."

Be resilient and strong for there is more to come. Stay positive and faithful. Faith is an indispensable force that fuels human spirit.

Be aware of what you engage in. Behind one there is always another that may be bigger, badder, stronger, or harder.

SCAN QR CODE FOR AUDIO & ILLUSTRATIONS

PROVERB, SAYINGS & ILLUSTRATIONS

Avan ou monte bwa gade si ou ka desann li.

"Before you climb the tree, make sure you can get down"

Before you start or engage in anything, think about the consequences. Many pitfalls and traps are avoidable with a little foresight.

PROVERB, SAYINGS & ILLUSTRATIONS

Piti piti zwazo fè nich li

"Little by little, the bird builds its nest."

Take on your challenges in steps. Do not rush.
Slowly but surely you will get there.

The national bird of Haiti is the Hispaniolan Trogon (Priotelus roseigaster), a striking and colorful bird known for its vibrant plumage and distinctive appearance. Its upper body is primarily green, with a deep red belly and a white undertail. This unique avian species is native to the island of Hispaniola, which Haiti shares with the Dominican Republic, and it holds a special place in Haitian culture and symbolism. The Hispaniolan Trogon's presence in Haiti's biodiversity reflects the nation's commitment to preserving its rich natural heritage.

SCAN QR CODE
FOR AUDIO & ILLUSTRATIONS

PROVERBS, SAYINGS & ILLUSTRATIONS

Tout tan tèt pa koupe ou espère mete chapo.

"As long as your head is attached, you can hope to wear a hat."

When you are lost, remember you are still here with a chance to change your circumstances. Hope is somewhere you can always start. It will fuel your dreams and aspirations. Hope paves the way to confidence.

SCAN QR CODE
FOR AUDIO & ILLUSTRATIONS

PROVERBS, SAYINGS & ILLUSTRATIONS

Si ou pote chay, ou dwe konnen ki pwa li.

"If you carry the load, you should know its weight."

If you want to know the true measure of something, engage the people closest to it. They know that issue intimately and can provide insights that no one else can.

Si ou gen yon sekrè, pa dil ba yon moun, paske ou pral gen de sekrè.

"If you are keeping a secret, don't tell anyone, because you will have another secret."

If you tell a secret you are creating another loose end to manage. Its better to keep it to your self.

SCAN QR CODE FOR AUDIO & ILLUSTRATIONS

PROVERBS, SAYINGS & ILLUSTRATIONS

Men anpil, chay pa lou.
"Many hands make light work."

The more we work together the easier things will be.

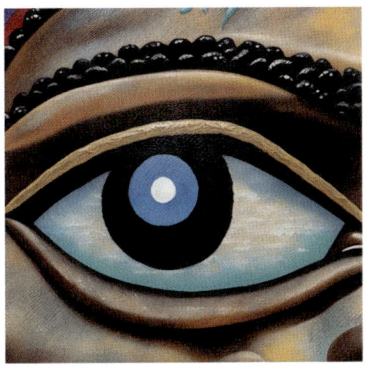

Lajan kase wòch.
"Money breaks rocks."

Money (or an incentive) can clear obstacles in your path.

SCAN QR CODE FOR AUDIO & ILLUSTRATIONS

PROVERBS, SAYINGS & ILLUSTRATIONS

Paròl gen zèl.
"Words have wings."

Words can travel faster than you can. Choose and use them wisely.

Zafè kabrit pa zafè mouton.
"The goat's business is not the sheep's business"

Everything is not for you, have discernment and mind what is your business.

SCAN QR CODE
FOR AUDIO & ILLUSTRATIONS

Haitian Food & Recipes

TASTES OF HAITIAN CUISINE

CAFE HAITIEN | HAITIAN COFFEE

Haitian coffee, often referred to as "Haitian Blue Mountain" coffee, is a hidden gem within the world of coffee connoisseurs. Grown on the lush, mountainous terrains of Haiti, this coffee offers a unique and rich flavor profile that sets it apart from its Central and South American counterparts. The beans are cultivated at high altitudes and nurtured by the country's tropical climate, resulting in a distinct combination of bright acidity and deep, earthy undertones. Haitian coffee's exquisite taste is often described as nutty with hints of chocolate and citrus, making it a delightful and complex cup of coffee that satisfies the palates of those fortunate enough to savor it. Beyond its flavor, the cultivation of Haitian coffee plays a vital role in the country's economy, offering employment opportunities and sustainability in an agricultural landscape that continues to evolve. A morning cup of coffee is often paired with buttered Haitian hard dough bread for a simple start in the morning or comfort food.

Some reputable Haitian coffee brands shipped worldwide include Caribbrew, Cafe Lux, & Cafe Kreyol.

CHOKOLA PEYI | HAITIAN HOT CHOCOLATE

Haitian hot chocolate, known as "Chokola Peyi," is a beloved and decadent treat deeply rooted in the country's culinary traditions. This rich and indulgent beverage is more than just a warm drink; it's a comforting embrace of flavors that reflects Haiti's vibrant culture. Made from scratch using locally sourced ingredients, Haitian hot chocolate features a base of finely grated cacao paste or cocoa powder mixed with spices like cinnamon, nutmeg, and cloves. The key ingredient that distinguishes it from other hot chocolates is the infusion of freshly grated mamba, a type of peanut butter unique to Haiti. This addition imparts a creamy and nutty essence, elevating the hot chocolate to a whole new level of deliciousness. Sweetened with granulated sugar or, more traditionally, pure unrefined cane sugar, it strikes a perfect balance between sweetness and the deep, earthy flavors of cacao. Served piping hot, often accompanied by fried or baked bread, Haitian hot chocolate is not merely a beverage but a comforting embodiment of the warmth, hospitality, and culinary creativity of the Haitian people. It's a cherished tradition that brings families and communities together, especially during festive occasions and chilly evenings.

Labouyi Bannann | Plantain Porridge

Haitian Labouyi Bannann, or Plantain Porridge, is a creamy and comforting breakfast dish made from ripe plantains and spiced with cinnamon, nutmeg, and vanilla. Here's a recipe to make Haitian Labouyi Bannann at home:

INGREDIENTS:

- 4 ripe plantains
- 4 cups water
- 1 can (12 ounces) evaporated milk
- 1 can (14 ounces) sweetened condensed milk
- 1 cinnamon stick (or 1/2 teaspoon ground cinnamon)
- 1/2 teaspoon ground nutmeg
- 1 teaspoon vanilla extract
- A pinch of salt
- Ground cinnamon and nutmeg (for garnish, optional)
- Freshly grated coconut (for garnish, optional)

SCAN FOR VIDEO RECIPE

INSTRUCTIONS:

1. **Prepare the Plantains:**
   a. Peel the ripe plantains and cut them into small pieces.
2. **Boil the Plantains:**
   a. In a large saucepan, bring 4 cups of water to a boil.
   b. Add the chopped plantains to the boiling water and cook until they are soft and easily mashed with a fork, about 15-20 minutes.
3. **Mash the Plantains:**
   a. Drain the cooked plantains and transfer them to a large mixing bowl.
   b. Mash the plantains with a fork or potato masher until they are smooth.
4. **Prepare the Porridge:**
   a. Return the mashed plantains to the saucepan.
   b. Add the evaporated milk, sweetened condensed milk, and the cinnamon stick (or ground cinnamon).
5. **Simmer and Spice:**
   a. Place the saucepan over low heat and simmer the mixture, stirring frequently to prevent sticking and lumps. This can take about 20-30 minutes.
   b. Stir in the ground nutmeg and vanilla extract.
6. **Adjust Consistency:**
   a. If the porridge becomes too thick, you can add more water or milk to achieve your desired consistency.
7. **Remove the Cinnamon Stick:**
   a. Remove the cinnamon stick if you used a whole one.
8. **Serve:**
   a. Ladle the Labouyi Bannann into serving bowls.
9. **Garnish:**
   a. If desired, sprinkle a pinch of ground cinnamon and nutmeg on top for extra flavor.
   b. You can also garnish with freshly grated coconut for added texture and flavor.
10. **Enjoy:**
    a. Haitian Labouyi Bannann is typically served warm and makes for a comforting and satisfying breakfast or snack.

Pate Haitien | Haitian Patties

Haitian patties, also known as "pâté haïtien" or "patty haïtien," are a delicious and savory puff pastry filled with seasoned ground beef, chicken or fish. They're a popular snack or appetizer in Haitian cuisine. This recipe gives you the basics of the Haitian beef patty. Tailor this to taste and swap in your favorite filling.

SCAN FOR VIDEO RECIPE

INGREDIENTS:

For the Dough:
- 2 cups all-purpose flour
- 1/2 cup cold water
- 1/2 cup cold vegetable shortening or butter
- 1 teaspoon salt
- 1 egg yolk (for egg wash)

* Use store bought puff pastry for a shortcut. (Not encouraged)

For the Filling:
- 1 lb ground beef
- 1 onion, finely chopped
- 2 cloves garlic, minced
- 1/2 bell pepper, finely chopped
- 2 tablespoons tomato paste
- 1 teaspoon thyme
- 1 teaspoon paprika
- 1/2 teaspoon cayenne pepper (adjust to your spice preference)
- Salt and pepper to taste
- Cooking oil for frying

Haitian beef patties are typically served as a snack or appetizer, but they can also be enjoyed as a light meal with a side of pikliz (Haitian pickled vegetables) or a salad. Enjoy your homemade Haitian beef patties!

INSTRUCTIONS:

1. **Prepare the Dough:**
   a. In a large mixing bowl, combine the flour and salt.
   b. Cut in the cold shortening or butter until the mixture resembles coarse crumbs.
   c. Gradually add cold water and mix until a dough forms. You may need a little more or less water, so add it slowly.
   d. Divide the dough into small balls, roughly the size of golf balls. You should get about 12 balls.

2. **Make the Filling:**
   a. In a skillet, heat a couple of tablespoons of oil over medium heat.
   b. Add the chopped onions, garlic, and bell pepper. Sauté until the vegetables are soft and fragrant.
   c. Add the ground beef to the skillet and cook until browned, breaking it apart with a spatula as it cooks.
   d. Stir in the tomato paste, thyme, paprika, cayenne pepper, salt, and pepper. Cook for an additional 5-7 minutes until the beef is well seasoned and cooked through. Remove from heat and let it cool.

3. **Assemble the Patties:**
   a. Preheat your oven to 350ºF (175ºC).
   b. Take one dough ball and roll it out into a circle about 1/8 inch thick on a lightly floured surface.
   c. Place a generous spoonful of the beef filling in the center of the dough circle.
   d. Fold the dough over to encase the filling and form a half-moon shape. Use a fork to crimp the edges and seal the patty.

4. **Bake the Patties:**
   a. Place the sealed patties on a baking sheet lined with parchment paper.
   b. Beat the egg yolk and brush it over the tops of the patties for a nice golden finish.
   c. Bake the patties in the preheated oven for 20-25 minutes or until they are golden brown.

5. **Serve:**
   a. Allow the patties to cool for a few minutes before serving.

Diri ak DJon DJon | Black Mushroom Rice

Haitian mushroom black rice, known as "Diri ak Djon djon," is a flavorful and traditional Haitian dish made with black mushrooms and black rice. These mushrooms give the rice a unique earthy flavor and a beautiful dark color.

SCAN FOR VIDEO RECIPE

Enjoy your homemade Haitian mushroom black rice! It's a delicious and unique dish that showcases the rich flavours of Haitian cuisine.

INGREDIENTS:

- 2 cups black rice (also known as "djon djon rice")
- 1 cup dried black mushrooms (djon djon mushrooms)
- 4 cups water
- 2 tablespoons vegetable oil
- 1 onion, finely chopped
- 2 cloves garlic, minced
- 1 bell pepper, finely chopped
- 2 sprigs fresh thyme or 1 teaspoon dried thyme
- 2 whole cloves
- Salt and black pepper to taste

INSTRUCTIONS:

1. **Prepare the Djon Djon Mushrooms:**
    a. Rinse the dried black mushrooms (djon djon mushrooms) to remove any dirt or debris.
    b. In a large pot, bring 4 cups of water to a boil. Add the mushrooms and let them boil for about 10 minutes.
    c. Remove the pot from heat and let the mushrooms steep in the hot water for at least 30 minutes or until the water turns dark and the mushrooms are soft.
    d. Strain the mushrooms, reserving the dark liquid (djon djon broth). Discard any tough stems from the mushrooms and roughly chop them.
2. **2. Cook the Black Rice:**
    a. In a large saucepan, heat the vegetable oil over medium heat.
    b. Add the chopped onions, garlic, and bell pepper. Sauté until the vegetables are soft and fragrant, about 5 minutes.
    c. Add the black rice to the saucepan and stir to coat it with the vegetables and oil.
    d. Pour in 3 cups of the reserved djon djon broth (the liquid from soaking the mushrooms). If you don't have enough broth, you can top it up with regular water to make a total of 3 cups.
    e. Add the thyme, cloves, and chopped djon djon mushrooms.
    f. Season with salt and black pepper to taste. Be cautious with the salt, as the djon djon mushrooms can be quite salty.
    g. Bring the mixture to a boil, then reduce the heat to low, cover the saucepan, and simmer for about 30-35 minutes or until the rice is cooked and has absorbed the liquid.
3. **Serve:**
    a. Once the rice is cooked, fluff it with a fork to separate the grains.
    b. Remove the cloves and thyme sprigs if you used fresh thyme.
    c. Haitian mushroom black rice is traditionally served as a side dish with meat or fish dishes. It's a flavourful and aromatic accompaniment to a variety of Haitian meals.

Mayi Moulen | Haitian Polenta

Haitian Mayi Moulen, also known as Haitian cornmeal porridge, is a creamy and comforting breakfast dish enjoyed throughout Haiti. It's made from cornmeal and is often flavored with vanilla, cinnamon, and sometimes nutmeg. Here's a recipe to make Haitian Mayi Moulen at home:

INGREDIENTS:

- 1 cup fine cornmeal
- 4 cups water
- 1 can (12 ounces) evaporated milk
- 1 can (14 ounces) sweetened condensed milk
- 1 cinnamon stick (or 1/2 teaspoon ground cinnamon)
- 1 teaspoon vanilla extract
- A pinch of salt
- Ground nutmeg (optional, for garnish)
- Freshly grated coconut (optional, for garnish)

SCAN FOR VIDEO RECIPE

INSTRUCTIONS:

1. **Mix the Cornmeal and Water:**
   a. In a large mixing bowl, combine the fine cornmeal with 2 cups of water. Stir to form a smooth, lump-free paste.
2. **Boil the Water:**
   a. In a large saucepan, bring the remaining 2 cups of water to a boil.
3. **Add the Cornmeal Mixture:**
   a. Once the water is boiling, carefully pour in the cornmeal mixture while stirring continuously. This helps prevent lumps from forming.
4. **Simmer the Porridge:**
   a. Reduce the heat to low and let the mixture simmer, stirring frequently to prevent sticking and lumps. This can take about 20-30 minutes. The porridge should thicken and become smooth.
5. **Add the Milk:**
   a. Stir in the evaporated milk, sweetened condensed milk, and the cinnamon stick (or ground cinnamon).

6. **Continue to Cook:**
   a. Allow the porridge to cook for an additional 10-15 minutes, or until it reaches your desired consistency. If it thickens too much, you can add more water or milk to achieve your preferred thickness.
7. **Flavor with Vanilla:**
   a. Stir in the vanilla extract and a pinch of salt. Remove the cinnamon stick if you used a whole one.
8. **Serve:**
   a. Ladle the Mayi Moulen into serving bowls.
   b. If desired, sprinkle a pinch of ground nutmeg on top for extra flavor.
   c. You can also garnish with freshly grated coconut for added texture and flavor.
9. **Enjoy:**
   a. Haitian Mayi Moulen is typically served warm and makes for a comforting and filling breakfast or snack.

This delicious and creamy porridge is a Haitian staple and a wonderful way to start your day with a taste of Haitian cuisine.

Pikliz | Haitian Spicy Topping

Haitian pikliz is a spicy and tangy coleslaw-like condiment that is a staple in Haitian cuisine. It is vinegar based and typically served alongside many dishes, adding a burst of flavor and heat. Here's a recipe to make Haitian pikliz at home:

SCAN FOR VIDEO RECIPE

INGREDIENTS:

- 1 large cabbage, finely shredded
- 2 large carrots, grated
- 1 large onion, thinly sliced
- 2-4 Scotch bonnet peppers, thinly sliced (adjust to your preferred spice level, you can remove the seeds for milder heat)
- 1 bell pepper, thinly sliced (for color and milder flavor)
- 3 cloves garlic, minced
- 1 tablespoon salt
- 1 teaspoon black pepper
- 1 teaspoon dried thyme
- 1 teaspoon grated fresh ginger (optional)
- 1 cup white vinegar
- Juice of 2 limes or lemons
- 2-3 tablespoons olive oil

INSTRUCTIONS:

1. **Prepare the Vegetables:**
   a. In a large mixing bowl, combine the finely shredded cabbage, grated carrots, thinly sliced onion, thinly sliced bell pepper, minced garlic, and Scotch bonnet peppers. Wear gloves when handling Scotch bonnet peppers, as they can be extremely hot, and avoid touching your face.
   b. Sprinkle the salt over the vegetables and toss to combine.
2. **Make the Pikliz Brine:**
   a. In a separate bowl, mix together the vinegar, lime or lemon juice, black pepper, dried thyme, and grated ginger (if using). Stir until everything is well combined.
3. **Combine the Vegetables and Brine:**
   a. Pour the pikliz brine over the prepared vegetables.
   b. Drizzle the olive oil over the mixture.
   c. Use clean hands or gloves to toss everything together, ensuring that the vegetables are well coated with the brine.
4. **Pack and Store:**
   a. Transfer the pikliz into clean, airtight jars or containers, pressing it down to ensure there are no air pockets.
   b. Seal the jars or containers and store them in the refrigerator.
5. **Allow to Marinate:**
   a. Pikliz is best when it's allowed to marinate for at least 24 hours in the refrigerator. This allows the flavors to meld together and develop the characteristic tang and heat.
6. **Serve:**
   a. Haitian pikliz can be served as a condiment alongside a wide range of Haitian dishes, including grilled meats, fried fish, rice and beans, and more. Its spicy and tangy kick adds a delightful contrast to many dishes.

Keep in mind that Haitian pikliz is quite spicy, so you can adjust the heat level to your preference by using fewer Scotch bonnet peppers or removing the seeds and membranes for milder flavor. Enjoy your homemade Haitian pikliz!

Tablet | Sweet Crunchy Treat

Haitian tablet, also known as "Tablet Coco" or "Kònfiti," is a sweet and crunchy coconut confection that's popular in Haitian cuisine. It's made from simple ingredients and is a delightful treat.

SCAN FOR VIDEO RECIPE

INGREDIENTS:

- 2 cups grated coconut (fresh or desiccated)
- 2 cups granulated sugar
- 1/2 cup water
- 1 teaspoon vanilla extract (optional)
- A pinch of salt

Store any leftover Haitian tablet in an airtight container to keep it fresh.

INSTRUCTIONS:

1. **Prepare the Coconut:**
    a. If you're using fresh coconut, grate it finely using a grater. If you're using desiccated coconut, you can use it as is.
2. **Combine Ingredients:**
    a. In a heavy-bottomed saucepan, combine the grated coconut, granulated sugar, water, and a pinch of salt.
3. **Cook the Mixture:**
    a. Place the saucepan over medium-high heat and stir the mixture continuously.
    b. Continue stirring as the mixture cooks. It will start to thicken and turn golden brown. This should take about 15-20 minutes.
    c. You'll notice that the mixture becomes thicker and starts to pull away from the sides of the saucepan.
4. **Add Vanilla Extract:**
    a. If you want to enhance the flavor, you can add the optional teaspoon of vanilla extract at this point. Stir it in.
5. **Test for Doneness:**
    a. To test if the mixture is done, drop a small spoonful onto a plate. If it cools and hardens into a firm consistency, it's ready.
6. **Shape the Tablet:**
    a. Quickly pour the hot mixture onto a greased or parchment paper-lined baking sheet or into greased molds.
    b. Use the back of a spoon to flatten and shape the tablet. You can also use molds for decorative shapes.
7. **Allow to Cool:**
    a. Let the tablet cool and harden for about 1-2 hours. It should become firm and easy to handle.
8. **Break into Pieces:**
    a. Once the tablet is completely cooled and hardened, break it into pieces of your desired size.
9. **Serve:**
    a. Haitian tablet can be served as a sweet treat or snack. It's perfect for sharing with friends and family or as a delightful gift.

Akra | Malanga Fritters

SCAN FOR VIDEO RECIPE

Haitian akra, also known as malanga fritters, are a popular street food in Haiti. These crispy fritters are made from grated malanga root (similar to taro root) and seasoned with herbs and spices. Here's a recipe to make Haitian akra at home:

INGREDIENTS:

- 2 cups grated malanga root (about 1 large malanga root)
- 1/2 cup finely chopped scallions (green onions)
- 2-3 cloves garlic, minced
- 1/2 to 1 Scotch bonnet pepper, finely chopped (adjust to your spice preference)
- 1 teaspoon salt (or to taste)
- 1/2 teaspoon black pepper
- 1 teaspoon baking powder
- Vegetable oil for frying

INSTRUCTIONS:

1. **Prepare the Malanga:**
    a. Peel the malanga root and grate it using the fine side of a box grater. Place the grated malanga in a clean kitchen towel and squeeze out any excess moisture.
2. **Mix the Ingredients:**
    a. In a large mixing bowl, combine the grated malanga, chopped scallions, minced garlic, chopped Scotch bonnet pepper, salt, black pepper, and baking powder. Mix everything together until well combined.
3. **Heat the Oil:**
    a. In a deep skillet or frying pan, heat enough vegetable oil to submerge the fritters over medium-high heat. The oil should be around 350°F (175°C).
4. **Fry the Akra:**
    a. Take a spoonful of the malanga mixture and carefully drop it into the hot oil. You can shape it into a small patty if desired.
    b. Fry the akra in batches, making sure not to overcrowd the pan. Fry them until they are golden brown and crispy, about 3-5 minutes per side.
    c. Use a slotted spoon to remove the akra from the oil and drain them on a plate lined with paper towels.
5. **Serve:**
    a. Haitian akra is traditionally served hot and can be enjoyed as a snack or appetizer. It's often served with pikliz (Haitian pickled vegetables) or a spicy dipping sauce.
6. **Enjoy:**
    a. Serve your homemade Haitian akra while they're still hot and crispy.

Haitian akra is a delicious and flavorful treat, known for its crispy exterior and tender interior. It's a fantastic way to experience the flavors of Haitian cuisine.

Sos Pwa | Bean Sauce

Haitian Sos Pwa (Bean Sauce) is a hearty and flavorful bean sauce made from black beans and typically served with rice.

SCAN FOR VIDEO RECIPE

INGREDIENTS:

- 2 cups dried black beans
- 1 onion, chopped
- 2 cloves garlic, minced
- 1/2 bell pepper, chopped
- 1 celery stalk, chopped
- 2 sprigs fresh thyme (or 1 teaspoon dried thyme)
- 2 whole cloves
- 1 Scotch bonnet pepper (optional, for heat)
- 2 tablespoons olive oil or vegetable oil
- 6 cups water (for cooking the beans)
- Salt and black pepper to taste

INSTRUCTIONS:

1. **Prepare the Beans:**
   a. Rinse the dried black beans thoroughly in cold water.
   b. In a large pot, add the beans and 6 cups of water. Bring to a boil, then reduce the heat to low, cover, and simmer for about 1.5 to 2 hours, or until the beans are tender. Be sure to check the water level periodically and add more water if necessary to keep the beans submerged.

2. **Make the Sos Pwa:**
   a. In a separate large saucepan, heat the oil over medium heat.
   b. Add the chopped onion, garlic, bell pepper, and celery. Sauté until the vegetables are soft and fragrant, about 5-7 minutes.
   c. Drain the cooked beans and add them to the saucepan with the sautéed vegetables.
   d. Add the fresh thyme, cloves, and Scotch bonnet pepper (if using) to the saucepan.
   e. Season with salt and black pepper to taste.
   f. Stir everything together and cook for an additional 5-10 minutes to allow the flavors to meld.

3. **Blend the Sos Pwa:**
   a. Remove the saucepan from heat and let it cool slightly.
   b. Using an immersion blender or a regular blender, carefully puree the bean mixture until it reaches your desired consistency. If it's too thick, you can add a little water to thin it out.

4. **Serve:**
   a. Haitian Sos Pwa is traditionally served as a side dish with rice, often accompanied by fried plantains or meat dishes.
   b. If desired, you can garnish it with a drizzle of olive oil and some additional chopped fresh thyme before serving.

Soup Joumou | Squash Soup

Haitian Soup Joumou is a beloved and symbolic dish traditionally consumed on Haitian Independence Day, which falls on January 1st. It's a hearty pumpkin soup packed with a variety of vegetables and often includes beef or other meat. Here's a recipe to make Haitian Soup Joumou at home:

SCAN FOR VIDEO RECIPE

INGREDIENTS:

- 2 pounds beef stew meat (bone-in or boneless), cut into chunks
- 1 large pumpkin (about 5-6 pounds), peeled, seeded, and cut into chunks
- 2 tablespoons olive oil
- 1 large onion, finely chopped
- 4 cloves garlic, minced
- 2 leeks, white and light green parts only, cleaned and chopped
- 2 carrots, peeled and diced
- 2 turnips, peeled and diced
- 2 potatoes, peeled and diced
- 2 celery stalks, chopped
- 1 green bell pepper, chopped
- 2 scotch bonnet or habanero peppers, whole (adjust to your spice preference)
- 2 cloves
- 2 sprigs fresh thyme or 1 teaspoon dried thyme
- 1 bay leaf
- Salt and black pepper to taste
- Juice of 1 lime or lemon
- Water (about 8-10 cups)
- 1 cup pasta (macaroni or other small shapes)
- 2 tablespoons tomato paste
- Fresh parsley, chopped (for garnish)
- Scotch bonnet or habanero pepper sauce (optional, for extra heat)

INSTRUCTIONS:

1. **Prepare the Pumpkin:**
   a. Peel, seed, and cut the pumpkin into chunks.

2. **Brown the Beef:**
   a. In a large, heavy-bottomed pot or Dutch oven, heat the olive oil over medium-high heat.
   b. Add the beef chunks and brown them on all sides. Remove the beef from the pot and set it aside.

3. **Sauté the Aromatics:**
   a. In the same pot, add the chopped onion, minced garlic, and chopped leeks. Sauté for a few minutes until they become fragrant and translucent.

4. **Add Vegetables and Spices:**
   a. Return the browned beef to the pot.
   b. Add the diced carrots, turnips, potatoes, celery, green bell pepper, scotch bonnet peppers, cloves, thyme, and bay leaf.
   c. Season with salt and black pepper to taste.

5. **Cook the Vegetables:**
   a. Pour in enough water to cover the ingredients in the pot (about 8-10 cups).
   b. Bring the mixture to a boil, then reduce the heat to a simmer. Cook for about 45 minutes to 1 hour or until the meat is tender.

6. **Blend the Pumpkin:**
   a. While the soup is simmering, place the pumpkin chunks in a separate pot, cover them with water, and boil until they are very tender (about 20-25 minutes).
   b. Drain the cooked pumpkin and blend it into a smooth puree using a blender or immersion blender. Set aside.

7. **Finish the Soup:**
   a. Once the beef and vegetables are tender, remove the whole scotch bonnet peppers, bay leaf, and thyme sprigs if using fresh.
   b. Stir in the pumpkin puree, tomato paste, and the juice of one lime or lemon. Mix well.
   c. Add the pasta and continue to cook for an additional 10-15 minutes or until the pasta is tender and the soup has thickened slightly. If the soup is too thick, you can add more water to achieve your desired consistency.
   d. Taste and adjust the seasoning with salt and black pepper. You can also add Scotch bonnet or habanero pepper sauce for extra heat if desired.

8. **Serve:**
   a. Serve the Haitian Soup Joumou hot, garnished with chopped fresh parsley.

Haitian Soup Joumou is not only a delicious and hearty soup but also carries cultural significance in Haitian history. Enjoy this special dish as a celebration of Haitian culture and independence.

Kremas | Coconut Cream Liquor

Haitian Cremas, also known as Kremas or Cremasse, is a sweet and creamy coconut-based liqueur often enjoyed during celebrations and holidays in Haiti. It's a delicious and rich concoction flavored with spices and typically contains alcohol (often rum). Here's a traditional recipe for Haitian Cremas:

SCAN FOR VIDEO RECIPE

INGREDIENTS:

- 1 can (14 ounces) sweetened condensed milk
- 1 can (12 ounces) evaporated milk
- 2 cans (about 24 ounces) coconut milk or cream (preferably freshly squeezed)
- 1 cup white rum (adjust to your preference, or use less for a non-alcoholic version)
- 1/2 cup dark rum (optional, for added flavor)
- 1 teaspoon vanilla extract
- 1/2 teaspoon almond extract
- 1/2 teaspoon grated nutmeg
- 1/4 teaspoon ground cinnamon
- A pinch of salt
- 1-2 cups granulated sugar (adjust to taste)
- Zest of 1 lime or lemon (optional, for a citrusy twist)
- 1-2 whole cloves (optional)
- 1/4 cup water (for dissolving the sugar)

Please enjoy Haitian Cremas responsibly, especially if you choose to include alcohol. It's a delightful treat that captures the essence of Haitian celebrations.

INSTRUCTIONS:

1. **Prepare the Spice Mixture (Optional):**
   a. In a small saucepan, combine the water, cloves, and lime or lemon zest (if using). Bring the mixture to a simmer and let it cook for a few minutes. This step infuses the water with these flavors.
   b. Remove the saucepan from heat and let it cool. Strain the liquid to remove the cloves and zest, leaving you with a flavored water.

2. **Dissolve the Sugar:**
   a. In a separate saucepan, heat the sugar over low heat, stirring continuously until it melts and turns into a golden caramel color. Be careful not to let it burn.
   b. Slowly add the flavored water (or regular water if you skipped the spice mixture) to the caramelized sugar while stirring continuously. This will dissolve the sugar and create a syrup.

3. **Make the Cremas:**
   a. In a large mixing bowl, combine the sweetened condensed milk, evaporated milk, coconut milk or cream, white rum, dark rum (if using), vanilla extract, almond extract, grated nutmeg, ground cinnamon, and a pinch of salt.
   b. Gradually add the sugar syrup to the mixture, stirring continuously until everything is well combined and smooth.

4. **Adjust Sweetness and Flavor:**
   a. Taste the Cremas and adjust the sweetness or rum content to your liking by adding more sugar or rum if necessary.

5. **Chill and Serve:**
   a. Transfer the Cremas to clean bottles or jars with airtight lids.
   b. Seal the containers and refrigerate the Cremas for at least 4 hours, but it's even better when chilled overnight.

6. **Enjoy:**
   a. Haitian Cremas is traditionally served chilled in small glasses as a sweet and indulgent drink during special occasions and celebrations.
   b. Garnish with a sprinkle of ground cinnamon or nutmeg before serving, if desired.

Legume | Eggplant Stew

Haitian Legume, a traditional Haitian eggplant stew, is a hearty and flavorful dish made with a variety of vegetables and typically served with rice. Here's a recipe to make Haitian Legume at home:

SCAN FOR VIDEO RECIPE

INGREDIENTS:

- 2 large eggplants, peeled and diced
- 1/2 lb beef stew meat, cut into chunks (optional)
- 1/2 lb smoked sausage or salted meat, sliced (optional)
- 1/2 cup vegetable oil
- 1 onion, finely chopped
- 3 cloves garlic, minced
- 2 green bell peppers, chopped
- 2 tomatoes, chopped
- 1/2 lb cabbage, shredded
- 1 carrot, peeled and diced
- 1 small yam or sweet potato, peeled and diced
- 1 malanga root, peeled and diced (optional)
- 1 chayote squash (christophine), peeled and diced
- 1/2 cup spinach or watercress, chopped (optional)
- 1/2 cup lima beans (frozen or fresh)
- 1 teaspoon thyme
- 1 teaspoon paprika
- 1/2 teaspoon cayenne pepper (adjust to your spice preference)
- Salt and black pepper to taste
- Juice of 1 lime or lemon
- Water (as needed)

INSTRUCTIONS:

1. **Prep the Eggplant:**
    a. Peel the eggplants and dice them into bite-sized pieces. Place them in a bowl of water with a little salt to prevent them from turning brown. Drain and set aside.
2. **Brown the Meat (Optional):**
    a. In a large pot or Dutch oven, heat the vegetable oil over medium-high heat.
    b. If you're using beef stew meat, add it to the pot and brown it on all sides. If you're using smoked sausage or salted meat, add it and sauté until it's lightly browned. Remove the meat from the pot and set it aside.
3. **Sauté the Aromatics:**
    a. In the same pot, add the chopped onion and minced garlic. Sauté until they become fragrant and translucent.
4. **Add the Vegetables:**
    a. Add the green bell peppers and tomatoes to the pot. Cook for a few minutes until they start to soften.
    b. Return the browned meat to the pot (if using).
5. **Layer the Vegetables:**
    a. Start layering the vegetables in the following order: cabbage, carrot, yam or sweet potato, malanga (if using), chayote squash, and spinach or watercress (if using).
    b. Add the lima beans on top.
    c. Sprinkle the thyme, paprika, cayenne pepper, salt, and black pepper over the vegetables.
    d. Add the diced eggplant on the very top.
6. **Simmer and Cook:**
    a. Squeeze the juice of one lime or lemon over the eggplant.
    b. Add enough water to the pot to almost cover the vegetables.
    c. Cover the pot and let it simmer over medium-low heat for about 45 minutes to 1 hour, or until all the vegetables are tender.
7. **Serve:**
    a. Haitian Legume is traditionally served with rice. You can also enjoy it with bread or as a standalone dish.

Haitian Legume is a delightful and hearty stew that showcases the flavors of Haiti. It's a versatile dish that can be customized with your choice of vegetables and protein.

Griot ak Banan Fri | Fried Pork & Plantains

SCAN FOR VIDEO RECIPE

Haitian Griot ak Banan Fri is a classic and flavorful Haitian dish consisting of fried pork (griot) served with fried plantains (banan fri). It's a delicious and popular combination often enjoyed with Pikliz (spicy pickled vegetables). Here's a recipe to make Haitian Griot ak Banan Fri at home:

INGREDIENTS FOR GRIOT:

- 2 pounds pork shoulder or pork butt, cut into bite-sized pieces
- 1/4 cup lime or sour orange juice
- 2 cloves garlic, minced
- 1 Scotch bonnet pepper, finely chopped (adjust to your spice preference)
- 1 teaspoon salt (or to taste)
- 1/2 teaspoon black pepper
- 2 sprigs thyme (or 1 teaspoon dried thyme)
- 2-3 cups vegetable oil (for frying)

INGREDIENTS FOR BANAN FRI:

- 4-6 ripe plantains, peeled and cut into rounds
- Vegetable oil (for frying)

INSTRUCTIONS FOR GRIOT:

1. **Marinate the Pork:**
    a. In a large bowl, combine the pork pieces with lime or sour orange juice, minced garlic, chopped Scotch bonnet pepper, salt, black pepper, and thyme.
    b. Mix well to ensure the pork is coated with the marinade. Cover and refrigerate for at least 2 hours, or overnight for better flavor.
2. **Fry the Griot:**
    a. In a deep skillet or Dutch oven, heat the vegetable oil over medium-high heat.
    b. Once the oil is hot, carefully add the marinated pork pieces in batches, making sure not to overcrowd the pan. Fry until they are browned and crispy on all sides, about 8-10 minutes per batch.
    c. Use a slotted spoon to remove the fried pork pieces and drain them on a plate lined with paper towels. Repeat until all the pork is fried.

INSTRUCTIONS FOR BANAN FRI:

1. **Fry the Plantains:**
    a. In the same oil used for frying the pork, carefully add the plantain rounds in batches. Fry until they are golden brown and tender, about 3-4 minutes per batch.
    b. Use a slotted spoon to remove the fried plantains and drain them on a plate lined with paper towels.
2. **Serve:**
    a. Haitian Griot ak Banan Fri is traditionally served hot and is often accompanied by Pikliz (spicy pickled vegetables) and sometimes rice and beans.

References

Abidor, M. (Trans.). (n.d.). Constitution of 1801. Constitution of 1801 by Haiti 1801. https://www.marxists.org/history/haiti/1801/constitution.htm

Basquiat, J.-M., & Holzwarth, H. W. (2023). Jean-Michel Basquiat. Taschen.

Batalova, J., & Dain, B. (2023, November 8). Haitian immigrants in the United States. migrationpolicy.org. https://www.migrationpolicy.org/article/haitian-immigrants-united-states#:~:text=The%20United%20States%20was%20the,%2C%20and%20Brazil%20(33%2C000).

Atlanta Black Star. (2016, November 21). 20 celebrities you didn't know were of Haitian descent. Atlanta Black Star. https://atlantablackstar.com/2014/09/15/20-celebrities-you-didnt-know-were-of-haitian-descent/

Coto, D. (2022, October 11). Explainer: Haiti's troubled history of foreign interventions. AP News. https://apnews.com/article/caribbean-united-nations-haiti-puerto-rico-a907efcd4a1b6f4c29bcc7a17f2b4900

Dubois, L. (2018, December 6). Heroines of the Haitian Revolution. Public Books. https://www.publicbooks.org/heroines-of-the-haitian-revolution/

Ferguson, J. (1989). Papa Doc, Baby Doc: Haiti and the Duvaliers. Blackwell.

Fortune, J. (2020). Haitian Proverbs and Idioms (Pwovèv ak Idyòm (ekspresyon) Ayisyen). YouTube. Retrieved December 30, 2023, from https://www.youtube.com/watch?v=xpP5tYThE6k&t=1474s.

Geggus, D. P. (2014). The Haitian Revolution: A Documentary History. Hackett Publishing Company, Inc.

Gladstone, N. (2010, January 20). 10 celebrities you probably didn't know are Haitian. MTV. https://www.mtv.com/news/0g2ab2/10-celebrities-you-probably-didnt-know-are-haitian

The Haitian Times. (2021, April 1). Haitian-Americans are making their mark in the NFL. https://haitiantimes.com/2019/02/04/haitian-americans-are-making-their-mark-in-the-nfl/#:~:text=The%20current%20batch%20of%20Haitian,the%20families%20of%20Haitian%20origin.

Louverture, T. (n.d.). Laws of the French colony of Saint-Domingue. The Library of Congress. https://www.loc.gov/item/2021666967/

Traveling Haiti. (2023, January 2). Haitian proverbs. Traveling Haiti. https://www.travelinghaiti.com/haitian-proverbs/

Murray, L. (2010, January 26). Léogâne. Encyclopœdia Britannica. https://www.britannica.com/place/Leogane#ref1074945

NBA players from Haiti. RealGM. (2000, February 15). https://basketball.realgm.com/nba/birth-countries/8/Haiti

Nina, E. (2023, May 15). Major exports of Haiti. International Trade Council - Solving trade-related issues. https://thetradecouncil.com/major-exports-of-haiti/

Haiti Open (2020, October 31). Haitian music: History, genres, and more. Haiti Open, Inc. https://m.haitiopen.com/country/haitian-music/

Prezi.com. (2016). History of Haitian Music. Retrieved December 30, 2023, from https://prezi.com/rfawxgzqezsj/history-of-haitian-music/.

Rai, M. (2022, October 27). Black history month: The Inspirational Women Fighting for Haiti's future. Forbes. https://www.forbes.com/sites/mandeeprai/2022/10/26/black-history-month-the-inspirational-women-fighting-for-haitis-future/?sh=a9fdb6f71982

Schimmer, R. S. (1492, January 1). Hispaniola. Hispaniola | Genocide Studies Program. https://gsp.yale.edu/case-studies/colonial-genocides-project/hispaniola

Trade Administration, I. (2022, August 3). Haiti - market overview. International Trade Administration | Trade.gov. https://www.trade.gov/country-commercial-guides/haiti-market-overview

Tucker, P. T. (2020). Gran Toya: Founding mother of Haiti, Freedom Fighter Victoria "toya" montou. PublishNation.

TV, F. (2018). Emmanuel Sanon | Haitian Hero | 1974 World Cup. YouTube. Retrieved December 30, 2023, from https://www.youtube.com/watch?v=tQgEtW9aHzI.

Vallon, J. L. (2007). What you should know about Haitian music and the evolution of Compas Direct. AuthorHouse.

Share the wisdom!

Visit us at

WORLDOFWISDOM.STORE

Thank you for your support!

Made in the USA
Middletown, DE
12 February 2024